THE PRIEST, PASTOR AND LEADER OF THE PARISH COMMUNITY

Congregation for the Clergy

THE PRIEST, PASTOR AND LEADER OF THE PARISH COMMUNITY

BOOKS & MEDIA
BOSTON

ISBN 0-8198-5942-7

Vatican translation

Printed and published in the U.S.A. by Pauline Books & Media, 50 Saint Pauls Avenue, Boston MA 02130-3491.

www.pauline.org

Pauline Books & Media is the publishing house of the Daughters of St. Paul, an international congregation of women religious serving the Church with the communications media.

1 2 3 4 5 6 07 06 05 04 03 02

CONTENTS

INTRODUCTION

This "Instruction," addressed to all parish priests and their brother collaborators involved in the *"cura animarum,"* is being relayed to them through the kind offices of their bishops. The document must be seen in the context of a deep reflection and study, which has been ongoing for a number of years on this topic.

With the publication of the *Directories* on the ministry and life of priests and that of the permanent deacons, along with that of the interdicasterial instruction, *Ecclesiae de Mysterio* and the circular letter *The Priest and the Third Christian Millennium, Teacher of the Word, Minister of the Sacraments and Leader of the Community,* we find the resonance of the documents of the Second Vatican Council, especially *Lumen Gentium, Presbyterorum Ordinis,* the *Catechism of the Catholic Church,* and the *Code of Canon Law,* in an uninterrupted expression of the *Magisterium.*

The document follows the same track as the great missionary impetus of the *duc in altum,* which necessarily leads to the indispensable task of the evangelization of the third Christian millennium. For this reason, mindful also of the many recommendations produced by a worldwide consultation on this matter, it has appeared appropriate to seize this opportunity to present a doctrinal section with elements which will provoke a reflection on those fundamental theological values which impel toward missionary activity and which are sometimes somewhat obfuscated.

The relationship between the ecclesiological-pneumatic dimension, which touches directly upon priestly ministry, and that ecclesiological dimension, which helps in understanding the significance of specific function, has been highlighted.

This "Instruction" has the underlying purpose of directing particular affection toward those priests who carry out their precious office as parish priests and who, though beset by many challenges, are always in the midst of their people. The delicate and valuable office they hold provides the opportunity to offer greater clarity with regard to the essential and vital difference which exists between the common priesthood and the ordained priesthood. This, in turn, gives rise to a proper understanding of priestly identity and the essential sacramental dimension of the ordained minister.

As it has been the intent to follow the line indicated by the Holy Father in his allocution to the Plenary Assembly of the Congregation, which is particularly rich in its practicality, it appears helpful to append it here.

ADDRESS OF JOHN PAUL II TO THE PLENARY SESSION OF THE CONGREGATION FOR THE CLERGY, FRIDAY, NOVEMBER 23, 2001

Your Eminences,
Your Excellencies, Monsignors and Fathers,
Brothers and Sisters in Christ!

1. With great joy I welcome you, on the occasion of the Plenary Assembly of the Congregation for the Clergy. I cordially greet Cardinal Dario Castrillón Hoyos, Prefect of the Congregation, and I thank him for his kind words addressed to me in the name of all present. I greet the cardinals, bishops and the participants in your Plenary Assembly, which has focused on an important topic for the life of the Church: *the Priest, Pastor and Guide of the Parish Community*. Stressing the function of the priest in the parish community, one brings to the fore the centrality of Christ who should always be prominent in the mission of the Church.

Christ is present to his Church in the most sublime way in the Blessed Sacrament of the altar. In the Dogmatic Constitution *Lumen Gentium,* the Second Vatican Council teaches that the priest *acting in persona Christi* celebrates the sacrifice of the Mass and administers the sacraments (cf. n. 10). As my venerable predecessor Paul VI so aptly observed in his Encyclical Letter *Mysterium Fidei,* which followed the Constitution *Sacrosanctum Concilium,* n. 7, Christ is also present through preaching and the guidance of the faithful, tasks to which the priest is personally called (cf. *AAS* 57 [1965], 762).

2. The presence of Christ, which thus takes place in a daily and ordinary way, makes the parish an authentic community of the faithful. It is therefore of fundamental importance for the parish to have a priest as its pastor, and the title of pastor is specifically reserved to the priest. The sacred Order of the presbyterate represents the indispensable and irreplaceable condition for him to be appointed pastor validly (cf. *Code of Canon Law,* can. 521, § 1). Certainly, other faithful can actively collaborate with him, even full time, but because they have not received the ministerial priesthood, they cannot replace him as pastor.

What determines this singular ecclesial centrality of the priest is the fundamental relation he has with Christ, Head and Pastor, as his sacramental re-presentation. In the Apostolic Exhortation *Pastores Dabo Vobis,* I noted that "the priest's relation to the Church is inscribed in the relation which the priest has to Christ, such that the 'sacramental representation' to Christ serves as the basis and inspiration for the relation of the priest to the Church" (n. 16). The ecclesial dimension belongs to the substance of the ordained priesthood. It is totally at the service of the Church, so that the ecclesial community has an absolute need for the ministerial priesthood to have Christ the

Head and Shepherd present in her. If the common priesthood results from the fact that the Christian people are chosen by God as a bridge with humanity and that every believer belongs to this people, the ministerial priesthood is the fruit of an election, of a specific vocation: "He called his disciples, and chose from them twelve" (Lk 6:13–16). Thanks to the ministerial priesthood, the faithful are made aware of their common priesthood and they live it (cf. Eph 4:11–12); the priest reminds them that they are the People of God and makes them able to "offer spiritual sacrifices" (cf. 1 Pt 2:5), through which Christ himself makes us an eternal gift to the Father (cf. 1 Pt 3:18). Without the presence of Christ represented by the priest, the sacramental guide of the community, this would not be an ecclesial community in its fullness.

3. As I said before, Christ is present in the Church in an eminent way in the Eucharist, the source and summit of ecclesial life. He is really present in the celebration of the holy Sacrifice, and when the consecrated bread is kept in the tabernacle "as the spiritual heart of the religious and parish community" (Paul VI, Encyclical Letter *Mysterium Fidei, AAS* 57 [1965], 772).

For this reason, the Second Vatican Council recommends that "parish priests ensure that the celebration of the Eucharistic Sacrifice is the center and culmination of the entire life of the Christian community" (Decree *Christus Dominus,* 30). Without Eucharistic worship as its beating heart, the parish dries up. Here it is helpful to recall what I wrote in the Apostolic Letter *Dies Domini:* "Among the many activities of a parish, none is as vital or as community-forming as the Sunday celebration of the Lord's Day and his Eucharist" (n. 35). Nothing will ever be able to replace it. The Liturgy of the Word by itself, when it is really impossible to ensure the Sunday presence of a priest, is praiseworthy to keep the faith alive, but it must always keep the regular celebration of the Eucharist as the goal to be achieved.

Where a priest is lacking one must ask the Lord with faith and insistence to raise up numerous and holy laborers for his harvest. In *Pastores Dabo Vobis* I repeated that "today the prayerful expectation of new vocations should become an ever more continual and widespread habit within the entire Christian community and in every one of its parts" (n. 38). The splendor of the priestly identity, the integral exercise of the pastoral ministry united to the efforts of the whole community in prayer and personal penance, are the irreplaceable elements for an urgent pastoral activity to recruit vocations. It would be a fatal mistake to be resigned to present difficulties, and act as if we should prepare ourselves for a Church of tomorrow that some imagine as being almost without priests. In this way, the measures adopted to remedy the present scarcity, in spite of all good will, would be seriously harmful for the ecclesial community.

4. Moreover, the parish is a privileged place to announce the Word of God. It includes a variety of forms, and each of the faithful is called to take an active part, especially with the witness of a Christian life and the explicit proclamation of the Gospel to non-believers to lead them to the faith, or to believers to instruct them, confirm them and encourage them to a more fervent life. As for the priest, he "proclaims the word in his capacity as 'minister,' as sharer in the prophetic authority of Christ and the Church" (*Pastores Dabo Vobis,* 26). To fulfill this ministry faithfully, corresponding to the gift received, he "ought first of all to develop a great personal familiarity with the Word of God" (ibid.). Even though he may be surpassed in the ability to speak by non-ordained members of the faithful, this would not reduce his being the sacramental representation

of Christ the Head and Shepherd, and the effectiveness of his preaching derives from his identity. The parish community needs this kind of effectiveness, especially at the most characteristic moment of the proclamation of the Word by ordained ministers: for this reason the liturgical proclamation of the Gospel and the homily that follows it are both reserved to the priest.

5. Also the function of guiding the community as shepherd, the proper function of the parish priest, stems from his unique relation to Christ the Head and Shepherd. It is a function having a sacramental character. It is not entrusted to the priest by the community, but, through the bishop, it comes to him from the Lord. To reaffirm this clearly and exercise this function with humble authority is an indispensable service to truth and to ecclesial communion. The collaboration of others, who have not received this sacramental configuration to Christ, is hoped for and often necessary.

However, these cannot in any way substitute for the task of the pastor proper to the parish priest. The extreme cases of shortage of priests, which advise a more intense and extended collaboration of the faithful not honored with priestly ministry in the pastoral care of a parish, do not constitute an exception to this essential criterion for the care of souls, as is indisputably established by canonical norm (cf. *Code of Canon Law,* can. 517 § 2). In this controversial sector, the interdicasterial exhortation *Ecclesiae de Mysterio,* which I approved in a specific way, is a sure guide to follow.

In fulfilling his duty as guide, which is his personal responsibility, the pastor will surely obtain help from the consultative bodies foreseen by canon law (cf. *Code of Canon Law,* cann. 536–537); but these must remain faithful to their reality as consultative bodies. Therefore it will be necessary to guard oneself from any form that tends *de facto* to weaken the leadership of the parish priest, because the very structure of the parish community would be distorted.

6. I now turn my affectionate and grateful thoughts to pastors throughout the world, especially to those who work in the outposts of evangelization. I encourage them to continue in the mission of evangelization that is strenuous but precious for the whole Church. I recommend to each one to turn, in the daily exercise of pastoral care, to the maternal help of the Blessed Virgin Mary, seeking to live in profound communion with her. In the ministerial priesthood, as I wrote in the *Letter to Priests on the Occasion of Holy Thursday 1979,* "there is the wonderful and penetrating dimension of nearness to the Mother of Christ" (n. 11). When we celebrate Holy Mass, dear brother priests, the Mother of the Redeemer is beside us. She introduces us into the mystery of the redemptive offering of her divine Son. *"Ad Jesum per Mariam":* may this be our daily program of spiritual and pastoral life!

With these sentiments, while I assure you of my remembrance in prayer, I impart to each one a special apostolic blessing, which I gladly extend to all the priests of the world.

Joannes Paulus PP. II

Part I

THE COMMON PRIESTHOOD OF THE FAITHFUL AND THE ORDAINED PRIESTHOOD

1. Lift Up Your Eyes (Jn 4:35)

1. "I tell you, lift up your eyes, and see how the fields are already white for harvest" (Jn 4:35). These words of Our Lord well illustrate the immense horizon of the incarnate Word's mission of love. "For God sent the Son into the world, not to condemn the world, but that the world might be saved through him" (Jn 3:17). His entire earthly life, which was completely consonant with the Father's salvific will, is a constant manifestation of that divine will which desires the salvation of mankind and that all come to that salvation eternally willed by the Father. He has bequeathed this historical mission to the Church and consigned it in a special way to her ordained ministers. "Great indeed is the mystery of which we have been made ministers. A mystery of love without limit, for 'having loved his own who were in the world, he loved them to the end' " (Jn 13:1).[1]

---

1. John Paul II, Letter to Priests for Holy Thursday 2001 (March 25, 2001), 1.

The priestly ministers of Jesus Christ, invested with the character and grace of the Sacrament of Orders, and constituted witnesses and ministers of divine mercy, voluntarily undertake to serve all in the Church. In whatever social, cultural or historical circumstances, including contemporary society, heavily marked as it is by an ethos of secularism and consumerism which erode the meaning of Christianity for many of the faithful, the Lord's ministers should always be mindful of "the victory that overcomes the world: our faith" (1 Jn 5:4). Indeed, contemporary society affords an opportunity to recall the conquering power of faith and of love in Christ, and to be mindful that, notwithstanding difficulties and even a certain diffidence, the Christian faithful—as well as many non-believers—greatly appreciate, and depend on, the pastoral availability of priests. They expect to find that the priest is a man of God, just as St. Augustine says: "Our knowledge is Christ and our wisdom is also Christ. He gives us faith with regard to temporal realities and it is he who reveals eternal realities to us."[2] We live in an era of new evangelization and should therefore go and search out those who await the opportunity of encountering Christ.

2. In differing degrees, Christ transmitted his own quality of Pastor of Souls to bishops and priests through the Sacrament of Orders so as to render them capable of acting in his name and of representing his *potestas capitis* in the Church. "The profound unity of this new people does not mean that there are not different and complementary tasks in its life. Those whose task it is to renew *in persona Christi* what Jesus did at the Last Supper when he instituted the Eucharistic Sacrifice, 'the source and summit of the entire Christian life' (*Lumen Gentium,* 11), are linked in a special way to the first apostles. The sacramental

2. St. Augustine, *De Trinitate,* 13, 19, 24: *NBA* 4, p. 555.

character which distinguishes them by virtue of their reception of Holy Orders ensures that their presence and ministry are unique, indispensable and irreplaceable."[3] The presence of an ordained minister is an essential condition for the Church's life and not merely for her effective organization.

3. *Duc in altum!*[4] Every Christian who experiences the light of faith in his soul and desires to walk at the pace set by the Supreme Pontiff must try to translate into deeds this urgent and decisively missionary call. The pastors of the Church, whose sense of the supernatural allows for the possibility of discerning the ways in which God desires to guide his people, must especially understand this same call and implement it zealously and readily. *"Duc in altum!* The Lord invites us to put out into the deep, with trust in his word. Let us learn from the Jubilee experience and persevere in the task of bearing witness to the Gospel with the enthusiasm that contemplating the face of Christ engenders in us!"[5]

4. It is important to recall how the Holy Father understands the fundamental goals set out by him at the end of the Great Jubilee of 2000, and offered to the particular Churches for concrete realization. Inviting all the local Churches to undertake this task, the Pope pointed to the need to profit from the grace received, "by putting it into practice in resolutions and guidelines for action."[6]

---

3. John Paul II, Letter to Priests for Holy Thursday 2000 (March 23, 2000), 5.

4. John Paul II, Apostolic Letter *Novo Millennio Ineunte* (January 6, 2001), 15: *AAS* 93 (2001), p. 276.

5. John Paul II, Letter to Priests for Holy Thursday 2001 (March 25, 2001), 2.

6. *Novo Millennio Ineunte,* 3: loc. cit., p. 267.

This grace touches upon the Church's mission of evangelization which requires personal sanctity on the part of both her pastors and faithful, a fervent apostolic sense concordant with their specific states of life which imbues their responsibilities and duties, and an awareness that the eternal salvation of many depends on faithfully manifesting Christ both in word and in deed. Hence, there emerges an urgent need to give greater impulse to the priestly ministry in the local Churches, especially in parishes. Such should be based on an authentic understanding of the ministry and life of priests.

We priests "have been consecrated in the Church for this specific ministry. We are called in various ways to contribute, wherever Providence puts us, to the *formation of the community* of God's People. *Our task...*is to tend the flock God entrusted to us, not by constraint but willingly, not as domineering over those in our charge, but by setting them an example (cf. 1 Pt 5:2–3).... This is our way of holiness, which leads us to our ultimate meeting with the 'supreme shepherd' in whose hands is the 'crown of glory' (1 Pt 5:4). This is our mission at the service of the Christian people."[7]

2. Central Elements of the Ministry and Life of Priests[8]

a) Priestly identity

5. Priestly identity has to be seen in the context of the divine salvific will since it is a fruit of the sacramental action of

---

7. John Paul II, Homily on the Occasion of the Jubilee for Priests (May 18, 2000), 5.

8. Cf. Congregation for the Clergy, *The Priest and the Third Christian Millennium, Teacher of the Word, Minister of the Sacraments and Leader of the Christian Community* (March 19, 1999).

the Holy Spirit, a sharing in the saving work of Christ, and completely oriented to the service of that work in the Church as it unfolds in history. Priestly identity is three-dimensional: pneumatological, Christological and ecclesiological. This primordial theological structure of the mystery of the priest, who is a minister of salvation, can never be overlooked if he is adequately to understand the meaning of his pastoral ministry in the concrete circumstances of the parish.[9] He is the servant of Christ. Through him, with him, and in him, the priest becomes the servant of mankind. His very being, ontologically assimilated to Christ, constitutes the foundation of being ordained for the service of the community. Total commitment to Christ, aptly effected and witnessed through celibacy, places the priest at the service of all. The marvelous gift of celibacy[10] is clarified by, and draws inspiration from, assimilation to the nuptial gift of the crucified and risen Son of God to a redeemed and renewed mankind.

The very life and work of the priest—his consecrated person and his ministry—are inseparable theological realities. Their object is service in promoting the Church's mission,[11] which is the eternal salvation of all mankind. The reason for the existence of the priesthood is to be found and discovered in the mystery of the Church, the Mystical Body of Christ and the People of God journeying through history, which has been

---

9. In this sense, it is important to reflect on what John Paul II calls "a minister of Jesus Christ the Head and Pastor of the Church," Post Synodal Apostolic Exhortation *Pastores Dabo Vobis* (March 25, 1992), pp. 695–696.

10. Cf. Congregation for the Clergy, Directory for the Ministry and Life of Priests *Tota Ecclesia* (January 31, 1994), 59: Libreria Editrice Vaticana, 1994.

11. John Paul II, *Pastores Dabo Vobis,* 70: loc. cit., pp. 778–782.

established as the universal sacrament of salvation.[12] "The ecclesial community has absolute need of the ministerial priesthood so as to have Christ, Head and Shepherd, present in her midst."[13]

6. The baptismal or *common priesthood* of Christians, which is a genuine participation in the priesthood of Christ, is an essential property of the New People of God:[14] "You are a chosen race, a royal priesthood, a holy nation, God's own people..." (1 Pt 2:9); "[He] has made us a kingdom, priests to his God and Father" (Rv 1:6); "[Thou] hast made them a kingdom and priests to our God (Rv 5:10)...they shall be priests of God and of Christ, and they shall reign with him" (Rv 20:6). These passages recall Exodus and transfer what was said of the Old Israel to the New Israel: "You shall be my own possession among all peoples; for all the earth is mine, and you shall be to me a kingdom of priests and a holy nation" (Ex 19:5–6). They also recall Deuteronomy: "For you are a people holy to the LORD your God; the LORD your God has chosen you to be a people for his own possession, out of all the peoples that are on the face of the earth" (Dt 7:6).

> While the common priesthood is a consequence of the fact that the Christian people has been chosen by God as a bridge with mankind and involves every believer who has been inserted

12. Cf. Second Vatican Council, Dogmatic Constitution *Lumen Gentium,* 48.

13. John Paul II, Address to the Plenary Meeting of the Congregation for the Clergy (November 23, 2001): *AAS* 94 (2002), pp. 214–215.

14. Cf. Apostolic Constitutions, III, 16, 3: *SC* 329, p. 147; St. Ambrose, *De mysteriis,* 6, 29–30: *SC* 25ff., p. 173; St. Thomas Aquinas, *Summa Theologiae,* III, 63, 3: *Lumen Gentium,* 10–11; Decree *Presbyterorum Ordinis,* 2; *CIC,* can. 204.

into this people, the ministerial priesthood is the fruit of being chosen; it is the fruit of a specific vocation: "[Jesus] called his disciples, and chose from them twelve" (Lk 6:13–16). By virtue of the ministerial priesthood, the faithful are made aware of their common priesthood and actualize it (cf. Eph 4:11–12); the priest constantly reminds them that they are the People of God and prepares them to "offer spiritual sacrifices" (cf. 1 Pt 2:5), through which Christ himself makes of us an eternal offering to the Father (cf. 1 Pt 3:18). Without the presence of Christ, represented by the priest, who is the spiritual leader of the community, this would not fully be an ecclesial communion.[15]

In this priestly people, the Lord instituted a *priestly ministry* to which some are called so that they might serve the faithful in pastoral charity through the *potestas sacra.* The common priesthood and the ministerial priesthood differ from each other not only in grade but also in essence.[16] The difference between the two priesthoods is, therefore, not simply one of greater or lesser participation in the priesthood of Christ, but one of essentially different ways of participating in that priesthood. The common priesthood of the faithful is based on the baptismal

---

15. John Paul II, Address to the Plenary Meeting, loc. cit., p. 215.

16. Cf. *Lumen Gentium,* 10; *Presbyterorum Ordinis,* 2; Pius XII, Encyclical Letter *Mediator Dei* (November 20, 1947): *AAS* 39 (1947), p. 555; Allocution *Magnificate Dominum: AAS* 46 (1954), p. 669; Congregation for the Clergy, Pontifical Council for the Laity, Congregation for the Doctrine of the Faith, Congregation for Divine Worship and the Discipline of the Sacraments, Congregation for Bishops, Congregation for the Evangelization of Peoples, Congregation for Institutes of Consecrated Life and Societies of Apostolic Life, Pontifical Council for the Interpretation of Legal Texts, *Interdicasterial Instruction on Certain Questions Regarding the Collaboration of the Non-Ordained Faithful in the Sacred Ministry of Priests Ecclesiae de Mysterio* (August 15, 1997), Theological Principles, 1; AAS 89 (1997), pp. 860–861.

character, which is the spiritual seal of their having been claimed for Christ. It "enables and commits Christians to serve God by a vital participation in the sacred liturgy of the Church and to exercise their baptismal priesthood by the witness of holy lives and practical charity."[17]

The ministerial priesthood, on the other hand, is based on the sacramental character received in the Sacrament of Orders, which configures the priest to Christ so as to enable him to act in the person of Christ the Head, and to exercise the *potestas sacra* to *offer sacrifice and forgive sins.*[18] A new and specific mission is sacramentally conferred on those of the baptized who have received the grace of the ministerial priesthood: to embody Christ's triple office—prophetic, cultic and regal—as Head and Shepherd of the Church in the midst of the people of God.[19] In exercising their specific functions, they act *in persona Christi Capitis,* and consequently, in the same way, they act *in nomine Ecclesiae.*[20]

7. "Our sacramental priesthood, therefore, is both 'hierarchical' and 'ministerial.' It is a particular 'ministerium,' that is a 'service,' with regard to the community of the faithful. It does not, however, derive from that community nor from its 'call' or

---

17. Cf. *Catechism of the Catholic Church,* 1273.

18. Cf. Council of Trent, Session XXIII, *Doctrina de Sacramento Ordinis* (July 15, 1563); *DS* 1763–1778; *Presbyterorum Ordinis,* 2; 13; Decree *Christus Dominus,* 15; *Missale Romanum,* Institutio Generalis, 4, 5 and 60; *Pontificale Romanum,* de Ordinatione, 131, 123; *Catechism of the Catholic Church,* 1366–1372, 1544–1553, 1562–1568, 1581–1587.

19. *Pastores Dabo Vobis,* 13–15: loc. cit., pp. 677–681.

20. Cf. Second Vatican Council, Constitution *Sacrosanctum Concilium,* 33; *Lumen Gentium,* 10, 28, 37; *Presbyterorum Ordinis,* 2, 6, 12. Congregation for the Clergy, *Tota Ecclesia,* 6–12; St. Thomas Aquinas, *Summa Theologiae,* III, 22, 4.

'delegation.' Rather, the ministry is a gift for the community which comes from Christ himself and from the fullness of his priesthood.... Conscious of this reality, we understand how our priesthood is 'hierarchical,' that is, how it is connected with the power to form and govern a priestly people (cf. ivi), and how, precisely because of this, it is also 'ministerial.' We exercise an office through which Christ himself incessantly 'serves' the Father in the work of our salvation. Our entire priestly life is, and ought to be, deeply imbued by this service if we wish adequately to offer the Eucharistic Sacrifice 'in persona Christ.'"[21]

In recent times, the Church has experienced problems of "priestly identity," deriving sometimes from an unclear theological understanding of the two ways of participating in the priesthood of Christ. In some areas, these difficulties have progressed to the point of losing that profound ecclesiological balance which is proper to the perennial and authentic Magisterium.

At the present time, however, circumstances are such that it is possible to overcome the danger of "clericalizing" the laity and of "secularizing"[22] the clergy.

The generous commitment of the laity in the areas of worship, transmission of the faith and pastoral collaboration, in the face of shortages of priests, has tempted some sacred ministers and laity to go beyond that which is permitted by the Church and by their own ontological sacramental capacities. This re-

---

21. Cf. John Paul II, Letter to Priests for Holy Thursday 1979 *Novo Incipiente* (April 8, 1979), 4: *AAS* 71 (1979), p. 399.

22. Cf. John Paul II, Post Synodal Apostolic Exhortation *Christifideles Laici* (December 30, 1988), 23: *AAS* 81 (1989), p. 431; *Ecclesiae de Mysterio,* Theological Principles 4, loc. cit., pp. 860–861; *The Priest and The Third Christian Millennium,* p. 36.

sults in a theoretical and practical underestimation of the specific mission of the laity to sanctify the structures of society from within.

This same crisis of identity has also brought about the "secularization" of some sacred ministers by the obfuscation of their absolutely indispensable specific role in ecclesial communion.

8. In the Church, the priest, *alter Christus,* is the minister of the essential salvific actions.[23] Acting *in persona Christi Capitis,* he is the fount of life and vitality in the Church and in his parish by virtue of his sacrificial power to confect the Body and Blood of the Redeemer, his authority to proclaim the Gospel, and his power to conquer the evil of sin through sacramental forgiveness. The priest himself is not the source of this spiritual life. Rather, it comes from him who distributes it to all the people of God. The priest, anointed by the Holy Spirit, is the servant who enters the sacramental sanctuary: Jesus Christ crucified (cf. Jn 19:31–37) and risen, from whom salvation comes.

With Mary, Mother of the Eternal High Priest, the priest is aware that, with her, he is "an instrument of salvific communication between God and man," albeit in a different way: the Blessed Virgin through the Incarnation, the priest through the power of the Sacrament of Holy Orders.[24] The relationship between priests and the Blessed Virgin Mary is based not only on a need for protection and assistance but more so on an awareness of an objective fact: "the presence of Our Lady," that "operative presence with which the Church lives the mystery of Christ."[25]

---

23. Cf. *Tota Ecclesia,* 7.

24. Cf. Paul VI, *Catechesis* at the General Audience of October 7, 1964: *Insegnamenti di Paolo VI,* 2 (1964), p. 958.

25. Cf. Paul VI, Apostolic Exhortation *Marialis Cultus* (February 2, 1974), 11, 32, 50, 56: *AAS* 66 (1974), pp. 123, 144, 159, 162.

9. As a participant in the directive action of Christ, the Head and Shepherd of his Body,[26] the priest, at the pastoral level, is specifically empowered to be a "man of communion,"[27] government and of service to all. He is charged with promoting and maintaining unity between the members and the Head, and among the members. By his vocation, he unites and serves this double dimension of Christ's pastoral function (cf. Mt 20:28; Mk 10:45; Lk 22:27). For its development, the Church's life requires energies which can only be supplied by this ministry of communion, government and service. It requires priests who are totally assimilated to Christ, and whose vocation originates in full appropriation of Christ. It requires priests who, "in" and "with" Christ, live all the virtues manifested by Christ the Shepherd, and who are motivated by, and draw inspiration from, assimilation with the nuptial offering of the crucified and risen Son of God to a redeemed and renewed mankind. It requires priests who wish to be sources of unity and of fraternal offering of self to all—especially the most needy. It requires men who, recognizing that their priestly identity derives from the Good Shepherd,[28] internally live that image and externally manifest it in a manner immediately recognizable to all.[29]

The priest renders Christ, Head of the Church, present through the ministry of the Word which is a sharing in his prophetic office.[30] *In persona et nomine Christi,* the priest is minister of the evangelizing word, which calls all to conversion and holiness. He is minister of the word of worship, which

---

26. Cf. *Pastores Dabo Vobis,* 21: loc. cit., p. 689.

27. Ibid., 18: loc. cit., p. 684; cf. *Tota Ecclesia,* 30.

28. Cf. *Presbyterorum Ordinis,* 13.

29. Cf. *Tota Ecclesia,* 46.

30. Cf. *Pastores Dabo Vobis,* 26, loc. cit., p. 698; *Tota Ecclesia,* 45–47.

praises God's greatness and gives thanks for his mercy. He is minister of the word of the sacraments, which are the effective source of grace. In these multiple ways, the priest, with the power of the Holy Spirit, prolongs the teaching of Christ in his Church.

b) Unity of life

10. Because of the ministry entrusted to priests, which in itself is a holy, sacramental configuration to Jesus Christ, priests have a further reason to strive for holiness.[31] This does not mean that the holiness to which the priest is called is in any way subjectively greater than that to which all the faithful are called in virtue of Baptism. While holiness takes different forms,[32] holiness is always the same.[33] The priest, however, is motivated to strive for holiness for a different reason: so as to be worthy of that new grace which has marked him so that he can represent the person of Christ, Head and Shepherd, and thereby become a living instrument in the work of salvation.[34] In fulfilling his ministry, consequently, he who is *"sacerdos in aeternum"* must strive to follow the example of the Lord in all things by uniting himself with him "in discovering the Father's will, and in the gift of himself to he flock."[35] *Unity of life,*[36] or *interior unity*[37] between the spiritual life and ministerial activity, is founded on

31. Cf. *Presbyterorum Ordinis,* 12; *Code of Canon Law (CIC),* can. 276, § 1.

32. Cf. St. Francis de Sales, *Introduction to the Devout Life,* part 1, chapter 3.

33. Cf. *Lumen Gentium,* 41.

34. Cf. *Presbyterorum Ordinis,* 12; *CIC,* can. 276, § 1.

35. Cf. *Presbyterorum Ordinis,* 14.

36. Cf. ibid.

37. Cf. *Pastores Dabo Vobis,* 72: loc. cit., p. 786.

love for the divine will and pastoral charity. Growth in this unity of life, founded on pastoral charity,[38] is promoted by a solid prayer life, so much so that the priest becomes, at one and the same time, a witness to charity and a master of the spiritual life.

11. The Church's history is redolent with splendid models of truly radical pastoral self-sacrifice. These include a great number of holy priests who have reached sanctity through generous and indefatigable dedication to the care of souls, commitment to asceticism and a profound spiritual life, among them the Curé of Ars, patron of parish priests. These pastors, consumed by the love of Christ and its attendant pastoral charity, are a lived expression of the Gospel.

Some currents in contemporary culture regard interior virtue, mortification and spirituality as forms of introspection, alienation or egoism, which are incapable of understanding the problems of the world and of people. In some instance, this has led to a multifarious image of the priest: it ranges from the sociologist to the therapist, from the politician to the manager. It has even led to the idea of the "retired" priest. In this context, it has to be recalled that the priest is a full-time bearer of an ontological consecration. His basic identity has to be sought in the character which has been conferred on him by the Sacrament of Holy Orders and from which pastoral grace derives. The priest, therefore, must always know what he has to do, precisely as a priest. As St. John Bosco says, the priest is a priest at the altar; he is a priest in the confessional; he is a priest in the school; he is a priest on the street; indeed, he is a priest everywhere. In certain contemporary situations, some priests are led to believe that their ministry is peripheral to life,

---

38. Ibid.

whereas, in reality, it is at the very center of life since it has the capacity to enlighten, reconcile and renew all things.

It can happen that some priests, having begun their ministry full of enthusiasm and ideals, experience disaffection, disillusionment or even failure. There are multiple reasons for this phenomenon: deficient formation, lack of fraternity in diocesan presbyterates, personal isolation, or lack of support from the bishop[39] and the community, personal problems, health, bitterness at not being able to find responses or solutions to problems, diffidence with regard to the ascetical life, abandonment of the spiritual life or even lack of faith.

Indeed, a dynamic ministry that is not based on a solid priestly spirituality quickly becomes an empty activity devoid of any prophetic character. Clearly, the disintegration of the priest's internal unity results, in the first place, from the decline of his pastoral charity, which amounts to a decline in "that vigilant love for the mystery that he bears within his heart for the good of the Church and of mankind."[40]

Spending time in intimate conversation with, and adoration of, the Good Shepherd, present in the Most Blessed Sacrament of the altar, is a pastoral priority far superior to any other. Every priest, who is a leader of his community, should attend to this priority so as to ensure that he does not become spiritually

39. *Christus Dominus,* 16: "His [the bishop's] priests, who assume a part of his duties and concerns, and who are ceaselessly devoted to their work, should be the objects of his particular affection. He should regard them as sons and friends. He should always be ready to listen to them and cultivate an atmosphere of easy familiarity with them, thus facilitating the pastoral work of the entire diocese. A bishop should be solicitous for the welfare—spiritual, intellectual, and material—of his priests, so that they may live holy and pious lives, and exercise a faithful and fruitful ministry."

40. *Pastores Dabo Vobis,* 72: loc. cit., p. 787.

barren, nor transformed into a dry channel no longer capable of offering anything to anyone.

Spirituality is, without doubt, the most important pastoral concern. Any pastoral initiative, missionary program, or effort at evangelization that eschews the primacy of spirituality and divine worship is doomed to failure.

c) The specific journey to holiness

12. The ministerial priesthood, to the extent that it conforms to the life and priestly work of Christ, introduces a new dimension to the spiritual life of those who receive this most precious gift. It is a spiritual life based on participation in the *gratia capitalis* of Christ in his Church, which matures through ministerial service to the Church: it is a holiness in ministry and through ministry.

13. Deepening "awareness that one is a minister of Jesus Christ"[41] is, therefore, of vital importance for the spiritual life of the priest and for the effectiveness of his very ministry. Ministerial relationship with Jesus Christ "gives rise to, and requires in the priest, the further bond which comes from his 'intention,' that is, from a conscious and free choice to do in his ministerial activities what the Church intends to do."[42] The phrase "to do in his ministerial activities what the Church intends to do" is enlightening for the spiritual life of all sacred ministers and invites them to a greater appreciation of personal instrumentality in the service of Christ and the Church, and to give that expression concrete expression through their ministerial activity. "Intention," in this sense, necessarily implies a relationship

---

41. Ibid., 25: loc. cit., p. 695.
42. Ibid.

with the actions of Christ in, and through, the Church. It also implies obedience to his will, fidelity to his commands, and docility to his actions: the sacred ministry is the instrument through which Christ and his Body, the Church, operate.

This is a permanent personal disposition: "This bond tends by its very nature to become as extensive and profound as possible, affecting one's way of thinking, feeling and life itself: in other words, creating a series of moral and spiritual 'dispositions' which correspond to the ministerial actions performed by the priest."[43]

Priestly spirituality requires a climate of proximity to the Lord Jesus Christ, of friendship and personal encounter with him, of "shared" ministerial mission, of love for and service to his Person in the "person" of his Body and Spouse, which is the Church. To live the Church and give oneself to her ministerial service implies a profound love for the Lord Jesus Christ. "This pastoral charity flows especially from the Eucharistic Sacrifice. This sacrifice is therefore the center and root of the whole life of the priest, so that the priestly soul strives to make its own what is enacted on the altar. But this cannot be achieved except through priests themselves penetrating more intimately through prayer into the mystery of Christ."[44]

In penetrating that mystery, the Blessed Virgin Mary, united with the Redeemer, comes to our assistance because "when we celebrate the Holy Mass, the Mother of the Son of God is in our midst and introduces us to the mystery of his redemptive sacrifice. Thus, she is the mediatrix of all the grace flowing from this sacrifice to the Church and to all the faith-

---

43. Ibid.

44. *Presbyterorum Ordinis,* 14.

ful."[45] Indeed, "Mary was associated with the priestly sacrifice of Christ in a singular way by sharing his will to save the world through the cross. She was the first and perfect spiritual participant in his oblation as *Sacerdos et Hostia*. As such, she can obtain and give to those who share ministerially in the priesthood of her Son the grace to respond all the more to the demands of the spiritual sacrifice which the priesthood demands: in particular she can obtain and give the grace of faith, hope and perseverance in the face of trials which stimulate a more generous participation in the redemptive sacrifice."[46]

For the priest, the Eucharist must occupy "the truly central place both in his ministry and in his spiritual life,"[47] because all of the Church's spiritual good derives from the Eucharist, which per se is the source and summit of all evangelization.[48] Hence, the importance of proper preparation before offering the Holy Sacrifice of the Mass, of its daily celebration,[49] of thanksgiving and of the visit to the Blessed Sacrament during the course of the day.

14. In addition to daily celebration of the Eucharistic Sacrifice, the priest prays the Liturgy of the Hours, an obligation he freely undertook *sub grave*. The priest intensifies his love for the divine Shepherd and makes him present to the faithful from

45. John Paul II, Introduction to the Mass celebrated on the liturgical memorial of Our Lady of Czestochowa, *L'Osservatore Romano,* August 26, 2001.

46. John Paul II, *Catechesis* at the General Audience of June 30, 1993, *Mary Is the Mother of the Eternal High Priest, L'Osservatore Romano,* June 30—July 1, 1993.

47. *Pastores Dabo Vobis,* 26: loc. cit., p. 699.

48. *Presbyterorum Ordinis,* 5.

49. Ibid., 13; *CIC,* cann. 904, 909.

the immolation of Christ on the altar to the celebration of the Divine Office with the entire Church. The priest has received the privilege of "speaking to God in the name of all," indeed of becoming almost "the mouth of the Church."[50] In the Divine Office he supplies what is lacking in the praise of Christ and, as an accredited ambassador, his intercession for the salvation of the world is numbered among the most effective.[51]

d) Fidelity of the priest to ecclesiastical discipline

15. An "awareness of being a minister" implies an awareness of the organic action of the Body of Christ. In order to make progress, the life and mission of the Church requires order, rules and laws governing conduct—in short, a disciplinary regime. Prejudice against ecclesiastical discipline has to be overcome, beginning with the very expression itself. Fear of citing ecclesiastical discipline or requiring the fulfillment of its demands must also be overcome. When the norms of ecclesiastical discipline are observed, tensions are avoided, which otherwise would compromise the unitary pastoral effectiveness which the Church needs so as to fulfill her mission of evangelization. A mature appropriation of one's own ministerial responsibilities takes it for granted that the Church, "organized as a social and visible structure...must also have norms: in order that its hierarchical and organic structure be visible; in order that the exercise of the functions divinely entrusted to it, especially that

50. St. Bernardine of Siena, *Sermo XX: Opera Omnia,* Venetiis 1591, p. 132.

51. Blessed Columba Marmion, *Le Christ idéal du pretre,* cap. 14: Maredsous, 1951.

of sacred power and of the administration of the sacraments, may be adequately organized."[52]

Consciousness of being a minister of Jesus Christ, and of his Mystical Body, also implies fidelity to the Church's will as concretely expressed in the norms of law.[53] The objective of the Church's legislation is the greater perfection of the Christian life so as to better accomplish her saving mission. That legislation should therefore be observed with sincerity and good will.

Among the various aspects of ecclesiastical discipline, docility to the Church's liturgical laws and dispositions, that is to say, fidelity to the norms which organize divine worship in accordance with the will of the Eternal High Priest and of his Mystical Body, merits special importance. The sacred liturgy is an exercise of the priesthood of Jesus Christ,[54] a sacred action par excellence, "the summit toward which the activity of the Church is directed...[and] the fount from which all her power flows."[55] In this area, consequently, the priest should be even more aware of being a minister and of his obligations to act in accordance with the commitments he freely and solemnly undertook before God and the Church. "Regulation of the sacred liturgy depends solely on the authority of the Church, that is, on the Apostolic See, and, as laws may determine, on the bishop.... No other person, not even a priest, may add, remove, or change anything in the liturgy of his own accord."[56] Arbitrariness, sub-

---

52. John Paul II, Apostolic Constitution *Sacrae Disciplinae Leges* (January 25, 1983): *AAS* 75, II (1983), p. XIII.

53. Cf. ibid.

54. Cf. *Sacrosanctum Concilium,* 7.

55. Ibid., 10.

56. Ibid., 22.

jective expressions, improvisations, disobedience in the celebration of the Holy Eucharist patently contradict the essence of the Holy Eucharist, which is the sacrifice of Christ. The same is true of the celebration of the other sacraments, especially of the celebration of the Sacrament of Penance, through which those who are penitent and intend to amend their lives have their sins forgiven and are reconciled with the Church.[57]

Likewise, priests should be careful to promote an authentic and conscious participation of the laity in the sacred liturgy, since the Church promotes such participation.[58] There are functions within the sacred liturgy which can be exercised by the faithful who have not received the Sacrament of Orders. Other functions, however, are proper and absolutely exclusive to ordained ministers.[59] Respect for the different states of life, and for their complementary nature in the Church's mission, requires that all confusion in this matter be carefully avoided.

e) The priest in ecclesial communion

16. In order to serve the Church, which is an organically structured community of the faithful invested with the same baptismal dignity and a diversity of charisms and functions, it is necessary to know and love her as she is willed by Jesus Christ, her founder, and not as passing philosophies or different ideologies would fashion her. The ministerial function of service to

---

57. Cf. *CIC*, can. 959.

58. Ibid., 23.

59. *Ecclesiae de Mysterio,* Theological Principles, 3; Practical Provisions arts. 6 and 8: loc. cit., pp. 859, 869, 870–872; Pontifical Council for the Interpretation of Legal Texts, Reply (July 11, 1992): *AAS* 86 (1994), pp. 541–542.

the community, which is based on configuration with Christ, demands a knowledge of and respect for the specific role of the lay faithful, and the encouragement of every possible means of having all assume their proper responsibilities. The priest is at the service of the community. He is also sustained by his community. He needs the specific contribution of the laity not only for the organization and administration of the community, but also for faith and charity: a certain osmosis exists between the faith of the priest and that of the other faithful. Christian families and fervent communities have often assisted their priests in times of crisis. It is likewise highly important for the priest to know, esteem and respect the nature of following Christ in the consecrated life, which is a precious treasure of the Church and a witness to the work of the Holy Spirit in her.

To the extent that priests are living signs and servants of ecclesial communion, they become part of the living unity of the Church in time, that is, of Sacred Tradition, of which the Magisterium is the custodian and guarantor. Reference to Tradition invests the ministry of priests with a solid basis and an objectivity of testimony to the Truth, which came in Christ and was revealed in history. This helps to avoid a prurience with regard to novelty, which injures communion and evacuates the depth and credibility of the priestly ministry.

The parish priest is called to be a patient builder of communion between his own parish and the local Church, and the universal Church. He should be a model of adherence to the perennial Magisterium of the Church and to its discipline.

f) Sense of the universal in the particular

17. "The priest needs to be aware that his 'being in a particular Church' constitutes by its very nature a significant

element in his living a Christian spirituality. In this sense, the priest finds precisely in his belonging and dedication to the particular Church a wealth of meaning, criteria for discernment and action which shape both his pastoral discernment and his spiritual life."[60] This is an important point which should be clearly understood in a manner which takes account of how "membership in and dedication to a particular Church does not limit the activity and life of priests to that Church: a restriction of this sort is not possible, given the very nature both of the particular Church and of the priestly ministry."[61]

The concept of incardination, as modified by the Second Vatican Council and subsequently assumed into the Code of Canon Law,[62] overcomes the danger of too tightly restricting the ministry of priests not only in geographical terms, but especially in psychological and even theological terms. Belonging to one particular Church and to the pastoral service of her internal communion, which are ecclesiological elements, also essen-

---

60. *Pastores Dabo Vobis,* 31: loc. cit., p. 708. "The *Church of Christ*—as *Communionis Notio* of the Congregation for the Doctrine of the Faith (May 28, 1992), n. 7, notes—is the universal Church...which is present and active amid the particular characteristics and the diversity of persons, groups, times and places. Among these manifold particular expressions of the saving presence of the one Church of Christ, there are to be found, from the times of the apostles on, those entities which are in themselves *Churches,* because, although they are particular, the universal Church becomes present in them with all its essential elements. They are therefore constituted *"after the model of the universal Church,"* and each of them is *"a portion of the People of God entrusted to a bishop to be guided by him with the assistance of his clergy" (AAS* 85 [1993], p. 842).

61. *Pastores Dabo Vobis,* 32: loc. cit., p. 709.

62. Cf. *Christus Dominus,* 28; *Presbyterorum Ordinis,* 10; *CIC,* cann. 265–272.

tially incorporate the life and activity of priests and lends them a specific structure consisting of determined pastoral objectives, goals, personal commitments to specific tasks, pastoral encounters and shared interests. In order to know and love a particular Church more effectively, to better understand membership of and dedication to her, to serve her to the point of giving one's own life so as to be sanctified through her, sacred ministers must always be aware that the universal Church "is a reality which is ontologically and temporally prior to every particular Church."[63] Indeed, the universal Church is not the sum total of all particular Churches. The particular Churches, in and with the universal Church, must be open to the reality of a true communion of persons, charisms, and spiritual traditions which transcends geographical, psychological or intellectual boundaries.[64] It should be perfectly clear to priests that the Church is one. Universality or catholicity should always pervade the particular. A profound, genuine and vital bond of communion with the See of Peter is the guarantee and necessary condition for this. Acceptance, diffusion, and conscientious application of papal documents, and of other documents published by the dicasteries of the Roman Curia, are its concrete expression.

Up to now we have given consideration to the life and work of all priests. Our reflection must now concentrate on those who have been specifically constituted as parish priests.

---

63. Congregation for the Doctrine of the Faith, Letter *Communio Notio* to the Bishops of the Catholic Church on Certain Aspects of the Church Considered as Communion (May 28, 1992), 9: loc. cit., p. 843.

64. Cf. Constitution *Lumen Gentium,* 23.

Part II

THE PARISH AND THE OFFICE OF PARISH PRIEST

The Parish and the Office of Parish Priest

18. The more important ecclesiological aspects of the theologico-canonical idea of parish were considered by the Second Vatican Council in the light of Tradition, Catholic doctrine, and the ecclesiology of communion. They were subsequently given canonical form in the Code of Canon Law. Post-conciliar papal teaching, implicitly or explicitly, developed them from various perspectives but always in reference to the ordained priesthood. A resumé of the main doctrinal, theological and canonical issues arising from this material will be useful especially in working out a more effective response to the pastoral challenges facing the parochial ministry of priests at the dawn of the third millennium.

By analogy, much of what is said in relation to the pastoral leadership given by parish priests also applies to priests who assist in parishes, as well as to those appointed to specific pastoral duties, such as chaplains in prisons, hospitals, universities and schools, and to those charged with the care of migrants and tourists, etc.

A parish is a specific community of the *christifideles,* established on a stable basis within a particular Church, whose pastoral care is entrusted to a parish priest as its own shepherd under the authority of the diocesan bishop.[65] Thus, the entire life of the parish, as well as the significance of its apostolic commitments to society, have to be understood and lived in terms of an organic communion between the common priesthood of the faithful and the ministerial priesthood; of fraternal and dynamic collaboration between pastors and faithful, with absolute respect for the rights, duties and functions of both, and mutual recognition of their respective proper competence and responsibility. The parish priest, "in close communion with his bishop and with his faithful...should avoid introducing into his pastoral ministry all forms of authoritarianism and forms of democratic administration which are alien to the profound reality of the ministry."[66] In this regard, the interdicasterial instruction *Ecclesia de Mysterio,* approved in *forma specifica* by the Supreme Pontiff, remains in full force. Its integral application assures that correct ecclesial praxis which is fundamental for the very life of the Church.

The intrinsic bond with the diocesan community and the bishop, and his hierarchical communion with the Successor of Peter, ensure the parochial community's membership of the universal Church. The parochial community is therefore a *pars dioecesis*[67] animated by the same spirit of communion, an ordered baptismal co-responsibility, a common liturgical life cen-

65. Cf. *Christus Dominus,* 30; *CIC,* can. 515, § 1.

66. *The Priest and the Third Christian Millennium,* p. 36; cf. *Tota Ecclesia,* 17.

67. Cf. *CIC,* can. 374 § 1.

tered on the celebration of the Holy Eucharist,[68] and a common missionary spirit shared by that community. Indeed, every parish "is founded on a theological reality, because it is a *Eucharistic community* (cf. Propositio 10). This means that the parish is a community properly suited for celebrating the Eucharist, the living source for its upbuilding and the sacramental bond of its being in full communion with the whole Church. Such suitableness is rooted in the fact that the parish is a *community of faith* and an *organic community,* that is, constituted by the ordained ministers and other Christians, in which the pastor—who represents the diocesan bishop—is the hierarchical bond with the entire particular Church."[69]

Thus, the parish, which is like a diocesan cell, should give "an outstanding example of community apostolate, for it gathers into a unity all the human diversity that are found there and inserts them into the universality of the Church."[70] The *communitas christifidelium* is the fundamental element of the parish. In a certain sense, the term underlines the dynamic relationship between those persons who, under the indispensable leadership of a proper pastor, are its constituents. As a general rule, such are all the faithful in a given territory, or some of the faithful in the case of personal parishes which have been constituted on the basis of rite, language, nationality or for other specific purposes.[71]

---

68. Cf. *Sacrosanctum Concilium,* 42; *Catechism of the Catholic Church,* 2179; John Paul II, Apostolic Letter *Dies Domini* (May 31, 1998), 34–36; *AAS* 90 (1998), pp. 733–736; *Novo Millennio Ineunte,* 35, loc. cit., p. 290.

69. *Christifideles Laici,* 26: loc. cit., p. 438; cf. *Ecclesia de Mysterio,* "Practical Provisions," article 4: loc. cit., p. 866.

70. Second Vatican Council, Decree *Apostolicam Actuositatem,* 10.

71. Cf. *CIC,* can. 518.

19. Another basic element for the idea of parish is that of the *cura pastoralis* or *cura animarum,* which is proper to the office of parish priest and principally expressed by preaching the Word of God, administering the sacraments, and in the pastoral government of the community.[72] In the parish, which is the normal context for pastoral care, "the parish priest is the proper shepherd of the parish entrusted to him. He exercises the pastoral care of that community under the authority of the diocesan bishop, with whom he has been called to share in the ministry of Christ so that, in the service of that community, he may discharge the duties of teaching, sanctifying and governing, with the cooperation of other priests or deacons and the assistance of the lay members of the faithful and in accordance with the norms of law."[73] The concept of parish priest is redolent of great theological significance while permitting a bishop to establish other forms of the *cura animarum* in accordance with the norms of law.

It recent times, it has become necessary to adapt pastoral care in the parishes to various circumstances such as shortages of priests in some areas, overpopulated urban parishes, depleted rural parishes, or parishes with reduced numbers of the faithful. This has required the introduction of certain innovations in the universal law of the Church concerning the pastoral care of parishes. Needless to say, these innovations do not involve any

72. Cf. Council Of Trent, Session XXIV (November 11, 1563), can. 18; *Christus Dominus,* 30: "Parish priests are in a special sense collaborators with the bishop. They are given, in a specific section of the diocese, and under the authority of the bishop, the care of souls as their particular shepherd."

73. *CIC*, can. 519.

innovations at the level of principle. Among such initiatives is the possibility of entrusting the pastoral care of souls, in one or more parishes, *in solidum* to several priests, on the condition that only one will act as moderator, directing the common pastoral activity of all, and personally assuming responsibility for it before the bishop.[74] On the basis of a multiple title, a single parochial office and the single pastoral care of a parish can be entrusted to several priests who participate in the office entrusted to them in an identical manner, and whose direction is personally undertaken by a brother priest who acts as moderator. Entrusting the pastoral care of a parish *in solidum* can prove useful in resolving difficulties arising in those dioceses in which reduced numbers of priests are obliged to distribute their time among several ministerial activities. It can also prove a useful way of promoting pastoral coresponsibility among priests and, in a special way, for promoting the custom of the common life among priests which should always be encouraged.[75]

It cannot, however, be prudently overlooked that pastoral care *in solidum,* which can only be given to priests alone, can give rise to certain difficulties. It is natural for the faithful to identify with their own parish priest. The continuing rotation of priests among themselves can be confusing or misunderstood in the parish. The great value of the spiritual paternity of the parish priest in his parish is clearly evident. The role of sacramental *"pater familias"* played by the parish priest, and its consequent ties, is pastorally effective.

74. Cf. *CIC,* can. 517 § 1.

75. Cf. *Christus Dominus,* 30; Decree *Presbyterorum Ordinis* 8; *CIC,* cann. 280; 550 § 2; *Tota Ecclesia,* 29.

In cases where pastoral necessity requires such, a diocesan bishop may entrust several parishes to the pastoral care of one priest on a temporary basis.[76]

Where circumstances require it, and as a provisional measure,[77] a parish may be entrusted to an administrator.[78] It should be recalled, however, that the office of parish priest, which is essentially pastoral, requires fullness and stability.[79] The parish priest must be an icon of the presence of the historical Christ. The demands of configuration to Christ underline the importance of this commitment.

20. The mission of pastor in a parish, which implies the full care of souls, absolutely requires the exercise of priestly orders.[80] Hence, in addition to ecclesial communion,[81] canon law explicitly stipulates that only a man constituted in the sacred order of the presbyterate can be validly nominated to the office of parish priest.[82]

---

76. Cf. Council of Trent, Session XXI (July 16, 1562), can. 5; Pontifical Council for the Interpretation of Legal Texts, *Nota Explicitiva,* published with the agreement of the Congregation for the Clergy, on those cases in which the pastoral care of more than one parish can be entrusted to one priest (November 13, 1997): *Communicationes* 30 (1998), pp. 28–32.

77. Cf. *CIC*, can. 526 § 1.

78. Cf. ibid., can. 539.

79. Cf. ibid., cann. 151, 539–540.

80. Cf. Third Lateran Council (anno 1179), can. 3; Second Council of Lyons (anno 1274), constitution 13; *CIC,* can. 150.

81. Cf. *CIC,* can. 149, § 1.

82. Cf. ibid., can. 521 § 1. Paragraph 2 of the same canon lists some of the principal personal qualities required in candidates for appointment to the parochial ministry: sound doctrine, moral integrity, zeal for souls and other virtues. Such candidates should have the qualities required by the general law of the Church in relation to clerics (cf. cann. 273–279) as well as those set out in particular law (those most necessary in a given particular Church).

With regard to the parish priest's duty to proclaim the word of God and to preach authentic Catholic doctrine, canon 528 explicitly mentions the homily and catechetical instruction; initiatives to promote the spirit of the Gospel in every ambit of life; the Catholic education of children and young people; as well as efforts involving the correct collaboration of the laity to ensure that the Gospel message reaches those who have abandoned the practice of the faith and those who do not profess the true faith,[83] so that they might come to conversion through the grace of God. Clearly, the parish priest is not obliged personally to fulfill all of these duties. Rather, he is obliged to ensure that they are discharged in his parish in an opportune manner and in conformity with the doctrine and discipline of the Church. These are realized as circumstances permit and subject to his personal responsibility. Some of the obligations incumbent on the parish priest must always be discharged exclusively by an ordained minister, as in the case of preaching during the celebration of the Holy Mass.[84] "Although he may be overshadowed by the eloquence of the non-ordained faithful, this does not erase the fact that he sacramentally represents Christ, Head and Shepherd, and the fact that the effectiveness of his preaching derives from this reality."[85] Other functions of the parish priest, such as catechesis, can be habitually carried out by the laity who have been properly trained doctrinally and who integrally live the Christian life. In such instances, the parish priest is obliged to maintain personal contact with these people. Blessed John XXIII wrote, "It is most important that the clergy

---

83. Cf. ibid., can. 528 § 1.

84. Cf. *Ecclesiae de Mysterio,* Practical Provisions, article 3, loc. cit., p. 864.

85. John Paul II, *Address* to the Plenary Meeting, loc. cit., p. 216.

are at all times faithful in their duty of teaching. 'In this respect, it is useful to hold and insist'—as St. Pius X says—'that priests are bound more gravely to no other office, nor more strictly to any other obligation.' "[86]

As is clear, the parish priest is bound by effective pastoral charity not only to encourage all of his collaborators but also to be vigilant in their regard. In some countries in which there are faithful who belong to diverse language groups, where no personal parish has been erected[87] nor adequate arrangements made for them, the territorial parish priest is the proper parish priest for such members of the faithful.[88] He is obliged to provide for their particular needs, especially in matters pertaining to their specific cultural sensibilities.

21. Concerning the ordinary means of sanctification, canon 528 stipulates that the parish priest is to give particular care to ensure that the Most Holy Eucharist is the center of the parochial community and that the faithful come to the fullness of Christian life by a conscious and active participation in the sacred liturgy, by the celebration of the sacraments, by the practice of prayer and by good works.

It is notable that the Code makes specific mention of frequent reception of the Holy Eucharist and of the Sacrament of Penance. This would indicate that the parish priest, in establishing the times for Masses and confessions in his parish, would take into consideration those times which are convenient for the

---

86. Blessed John XXIII, Encyclical Letter *Sacerdotii Nostri Primordia,* on the centenary of the blessed death of the Curé d'Ars (August 1, 1959), part III: *AAS* 51 (1959), p. 572.

87. Cf. *CIC,* can. 518.

88. Cf. Ibid., cann. 519, 529 § 1.

majority of the faithful, while bearing in mind also the need to facilitate those who have difficulty in easily attending the celebration of the sacraments. The parish priest should devote special attention to individual confession, understood in the spirit and form established by the Church.[89] He should be mindful that confession must precede first Holy Communion.[90] Moreover, the individual confessions of the faithful, for pastoral reasons and for the convenience of the faithful, may also be received during the celebration of the Holy Mass.[91]

Care should be taken to ensure respect "for the sensibilities of the penitent concerning the manner in which he wishes to confess, either face to face, or from behind a grill."[92] The confessor may also have pastoral reasons for preferring the use of a confessional equipped with a grill.[93]

The practice of visiting the Blessed Sacrament should be strongly encouraged. To this end, churches should be kept open for as long as possible, and their opening times fixed and established. Many parish priests promote the laudable practice of adoration of the Blessed Sacrament through solemn exposition and can attest to its fruits in the vitality of their parishes.

---

89. Cf. the "Propositions" on the parts relating to sacramental sign and form of celebration in John Paul II's Apostolic Exhortation *Reconciliatio et Paenitentia* (December 2, 1984), 31, III, 32: *AAS* 77 (1985), pp. 260–264; 267.

90. Cf. *CIC,* can. 914.

91. Cf. Congregation for Divine Worship and the Discipline of the Sacraments, in *Notitiae* 37 (2001), pp. 259–260.

92. John Paul II, *Address* to the Members of the Apostolic Penitentiary (March 27, 1993): *AAS* 86 (1994), p. 78.

93. Cf. *CIC,* can. 964 § 3; John Paul II, Motu Proprio *Misericordia Dei* (April 7, 2002), 9b; Pontifical Council for the Interpretation of Legal Texts, Reply circa can. 964 § 2 (July 7, 1998): *AAS* 90 (1998), p. 711.

The Blessed Sacrament is to be lovingly reserved in a tabernacle, "which is the spiritual heart of every religious and parochial community."[94] "Without the cult of the Eucharist, as with a beating heart, a parish becomes arid";[95] " 'If you wish the faithful to pray willingly and piously'—as Pius XII reminded the clergy of Rome—'set an example for them by praying in your churches before them. A priest on his knees before the tabernacle, with a proper disposition and in deep recollection, is a model of edification for the people, a reminder of, and an invitation to, prayerful emulation.' "[96]

22. Canon 529 elaborates the principal duties which are required for the fulfillment of the pastoral office of parish priest and outlines the ministerial characteristics expected of a parish priest. As the priest proper to the parish, he should make every effort to know the faithful entrusted to his care and avoid the danger of any form of functionalism. A parish priest is not a functionary fulfilling a role or providing services to those who request them. Rather, he exercises his ministry in an integral way as a man of God, seeking out the faithful, visiting their families, sharing in their needs and in their joys. He corrects with prudence; he cares for the aged, the weak, the abandoned, the sick, and the dying. He devotes particular care to the poor and the afflicted. He strives for the conversion of sinners and those in error. He encourages all in the fulfillment of the duties of their states of life and promotes the Christian life among families.[97]

---

94. Paul VI, Encyclical letter *Mysterium Fidei* (September 3, 1965): *AAS* 57 (1965), p. 772.

95. John Paul II, *Address* to the Plenary Meeting, loc. cit., p. 215.

96. *Sacerdotii Nostri Primordia,* part II: loc. cit., p. 562.

97. Cf. *CIC,* can. 529 § 1.

Promotion of the spiritual and corporal works of mercy remains a constant pastoral priority and a sign of the vitality of any Christian community.

Another important duty entrusted to the parish priest is the promotion of the proper role of the laity in the Church's mission, which is that of quickening and perfecting the temporal order with the spirit of the Gospel, thereby giving witness to Christ through the exercise of secular tasks.[98]

The parish priest is obliged to collaborate with his bishop and with the other priests of the diocese so as to ensure that the faithful who participate in the parochial community become aware that they are also members of the diocese and of the universal Church.[99] The increasing mobility of contemporary society makes it all the more necessary that the parish does not become introspective. Rather, it should welcome the faithful of other parishes and avoid discouraging its own parishioners from participating in the life of other parishes, rectories or chaplaincies.

The parish priest is particularly bound zealously to promote, sustain and follow vocations to the priesthood.[100] Personal example, given by visibly owning his priestly identity,[101] living consistently with it, together with devotion to individual confession, spiritual direction of young people, and catechesis on the ordained ministry are indispensable to any pastoral promotion of priestly vocations. "It has always been a special duty of the priestly ministry to sow the seeds of life totally consecrated to God and to promote love of virginity."[102]

---

98. Cf. ibid., can. 225.

99. Cf. *CIC,* 529 § 2.

100. Cf. *CIC,* can. 233 § 1; *Pastores Dabo Vobis,* 41: loc. cit., p. 727.

101. Cf. *Tota Ecclesia,* 66.

102. St. Ambrose, *De Virginitate,* 5, 36: *PL* 16, p. 286.

The Code attributes the following duties specifically to parish priests:[103] to administer the Sacrament of Baptism and that of Confirmation to those in danger of death in accordance with canon 883, § 3;[104] to administer Viaticum and the Sacrament of the Anointing of the Sick, without prejudice to the provisions of canon 1003, §§ 2 and 3;[105] to impart the Apostolic Blessing; to assist at and bless marriages; to celebrate funerals; to bless the baptismal font in Eastertide; to lead processions and impart solemn blessings outside of the church; to solemnly celebrate the Sacrament of the Most Holy Eucharist on Sundays and on the feasts of precept.

Rather than duties or rights given exclusively to the parish priest, these functions are entrusted to him in a special way in virtue of his particular responsibility as parish priest. They should consequently be discharged personally, insofar as possible, or at least overseen by the parish priest.

23. In those areas experiencing shortages of priests it can happen, as is already the case in some places, that the bishop, after prudent consideration, may entrust a certain *collaboration "ad tempus"* in the exercise of the pastoral care of a parish, in the canonically approved manner, to a person or persons who

---

103. *CIC,* can. 530.

104. Ibid., can. 883, 3°. "The following have the faculty of administering confirmation by the law itself.... 3° with regard to danger of death, the parish priest or indeed any priest."

105. Ibid., can. 1003, § 2: "All priests to whom the care of souls has been committed have the duty and the right to administer the anointing of the sick to all the faithful committed to their pastoral office; for a reasonable cause any other priest can administer this sacrament with at least the presumed consent of the aforementioned priest." § 3: "Every priest is allowed to carry the sacred oil with him so that he can administer the Sacrament of the Anointing of the Sick in case of necessity."

have not been invested with priestly character.[106] In such cases, however, the original properties of diversity and complementarity of the charisms and functions of ordained ministers and the lay faithful must be carefully observed and respected, since these are proper to the Church and are willed by God for its organization. Extraordinary situations exist which justify such collaboration. Such collaboration, however, may not lawfully supersede the specific nature of the sacred ministry and the lay state.

In her desire to clarify terminology that might occasion confusion, the Church exclusively reserves certain expressions connoting *"potestas capitis"* to priests—"pastor," "chaplain," "director," "coordinator" and other equivalents.[107]

In its title dedicated to the rights and duties of the lay faithful, the Code distinguishes between those competencies or functions which properly belong to all the lay faithful by right or duty, and those deriving from collaboration with the pastoral ministry. These latter are a *capacitas* or *habilitas* whose exercise depends on being called by the Church's lawful pastors.[108] Thus, they are in no sense, "rights."

24. The foregoing has already been clarified by John Paul II in the Post-Synodal Apostolic Exhortation *Christifideles Laici* (n. 23):

> The Church's mission of salvation in the world is realized not only by the ministers in virtue of the Sacrament of Orders but also by all the lay faithful; indeed, because of their baptismal state and their specific vocation, in the measure proper to each person, the lay faithful participate in the priestly, prophetic and kingly mission of Christ.

---

106. Cf. ibid., can 517 § 2.
107. John Paul II, *Address* to the Plenary Meeting, loc. cit., p. 214.
108. Cf. *CIC,* cann. 228, 229, §§ 1 and 3; 230.

The pastors, therefore, ought to acknowledge and foster the ministries, offices and roles of the lay faithful that find their *foundation in the Sacraments of Baptism and Confirmation,* and indeed, for a good many of them, *in the Sacrament of Matrimony.* When necessity in the Church requires it, the pastors, according to the established norms of universal law, can entrust to the lay faithful, *ad tempus,* certain offices and roles connected with their pastoral ministry which do not require the character of Orders. This same document recalls the basic principles underlying this collaboration and sets the limits for it: the exercise of such tasks does not make pastors of the lay faithful: in fact, a person is not a minister simply in performing a task, but through sacramental ordination. Only the Sacrament of Orders gives the ordained minister a particular participation in the office of Christ, the Shepherd and Head, and in his Eternal Priesthood. Supplying certain tasks by the laity takes its legitimacy, formally and immediately, from the official deputation given by the pastors to the laity, as well as from its concrete exercise under the guidance of ecclesiastical authority.[109]

In those cases where a collaboration with the ordained ministry has been entrusted to the non-ordained faithful, a priest must necessarily be appointed as moderator and vested with the power and duties of a parish priest, personally to direct pastoral care.[110]

Clearly, the office of parish priest exercised by a priest who has been designated to direct pastoral activity—i.e., one invested with the faculties of a parish priest—and exercise those functions which are exclusively priestly differs completely from the subsidiary collaboration of the non-ordained faithful

109. Cf. also *Presbyterorum Ordinis,* 2; *Catechism of the Catholic Church,* 1563.

110. Cf. *CIC,* can. 517 § 2; *Catechism of the Catholic Church,* 911.

in the other functions of the office.[111] A non-ordained male religious, a female religious or a lay person may exercise administrative functions, as well as that of promoting spiritual formation. They may not, however, exercise functions which belong fully to the care of souls since this requires priestly character. They may, nevertheless, *supply for the ordained minister in those liturgical functions which are consonant with their canonical condition* and enumerated in canon 230 § 3: "exercise the ministry of the word, preside over liturgical prayers, confer Baptism, and distribute Holy Communion in accordance with the prescriptions of law."[112] Even deacons, who cannot be equated with other members of the faithful, cannot exercise the full *cura animarum.*[113]

It is always advisable for the diocesan bishop to verify every case of necessity with the utmost prudence and pastoral foresight. He should establish criteria to determine the suitability of those called to this form of collaboration and clearly define the functions to be given to each of them in accordance with the circumstances of each respective parish. In the absence of a specific and clear assignment of functions, the priest moderator will determine in the matter. The exceptional and provisional nature of such arrangements require the promotion of an awareness of the absolute need for priestly vocations in these parish communities. The seeds of such vocations should be

---

111. Cf. *Ecclesiae de Mysterio,* "Theological Principles" and "Practical Provisions": loc. cit., pp. 856–875: *CIC,* can. 517 § 2.

112. *Ecclesiae de Mysterio,* Practical Provisions, articles 6; 8: loc. cit., pp. 869; 870 – 872.

113. Cf. *CIC,* can. 150: *Catechism of the Catholic Church,* 1554; 1570.

encouraged in them; community and personal prayer for vocations should be promoted as well as prayers for the sanctification of priests.

In order to ensure that priestly vocations may flourish more easily in the community, it is important that an authentic love for the Church should imbue it. A profound esteem and strong enthusiasm for the Bride of Christ, who collaborates with the Holy Spirit in the work of salvation, should always be promoted and encouraged.

Every effort, therefore, has to be made to keep alive in the hearts of the faithful that joy and holy pride deriving from membership in the Church which is so palpably evident in the first letter of St. Peter and in the Apocalypse (cf. 1 Pt 3:14; Rv 2:13, 17; 7:9; 14:1ff.; 19:6; 22, 14). Without this joy and pride, at a psychological level it becomes difficult to conserve and develop the life of faith. It is not surprising, at least at the level of psychology, that in some contexts priestly vocations fail to germinate or come to maturity.

"It would be a fatal error to despair in the face of present difficulties and adopt an attitude which, de facto, would prepare a Church of the future which would be almost bereft of priests. Measures adopted in this light to counter present shortages of priests, notwithstanding the good intentions motivating them, would, in fact, be seriously prejudicial for the ecclesial community."[114]

25. "Where permanent deacons participate in the pastoral care of parishes which, because of a shortage of priests, do not have the immediate benefit of a parish priest, they should have

114. John Paul II, Address to the Plenary Meeting, loc. cit., p. 216.

precedence over the non-ordained faithful."[115] In virtue of sacred orders, "the deacon is teacher insofar as he preaches and bears witness to the Word of God; he sanctifies when he administers the Sacrament of Baptism, the Holy Eucharist and the sacramentals; he participates at the Holy Eucharist as 'a minister of the Blood,' and conserves and distributes the Blessed Eucharist; he is a guide inasmuch as he animates the community or a section of ecclesial life."[116]

Deacons who are candidates for ordination to the priesthood should be especially welcome when they offer their pastoral services in a parish. In agreement with the seminary authorities, the parish priest should be a guide and a teacher, conscious that a sincere and total self-offering to Christ on the part of a candidate for the priesthood can depend on his own coherent witness to priestly identity, and to the missionary generosity of his service and love for the parish.

26. Like the diocesan pastoral council,[117] the provisions of law foresee the constitution of a pastoral council at the parochial level, should such be considered opportune by the bishop, having heard his council of priests.[118] The basic task of such a council is to serve, at the institutional level, the orderly collaboration of the faithful in the development of pastoral activity which is proper to priests.[119] The pastoral council is thus a

---

115. Congregation for the Clergy, Directory for the Ministry and Life of Permanent Deacons (February 22, 1998), 41: *AAS* 90 (1998), p. 901.

116. Ibid., 22: loc. cit., p. 889.

117. Cf. *Christus Dominus,* 27; *CIC,* cann. 511–514.

118. Cf. *CIC,* can. 561 § 1.

119. Cf. Ibid., can. 536 § 1.

consultative organ in which the faithful, expressing their baptismal responsibility, can assist the parish priest, who presides at the council,[120] by offering their advice on pastoral matters:[121] "The lay faithful ought to be ever more convinced of the special meaning that their commitment to the apostolate takes on in their parish"; hence it is necessary to have "a more convinced, extensive and decided appreciation for 'parish pastoral councils.'"[122] There are clear reasons for this: "In the present circumstances the lay faithful have the ability to do very much and, therefore, ought to do very much toward the growth of an authentic ecclesial communion in their parishes in order to reawaken missionary zeal toward nonbelievers and believers themselves who have abandoned the faith or grown lax in the Christian life."[123]

"All of the faithful have the right, sometimes even the duty, to make their opinions known on matters concerning the good of the Church. This can happen through institutions which have been established to facilitate that purpose: …the pastoral council can be a most useful aid...providing proposals and suggestions on missionary, catechetical and apostolic initiatives…as well as on the promotion of doctrinal formation and the sacramental life of the faithful; on the assistance to be given to the pastoral work of priests in various social and territorial situations; on how better to influence public opinion, etc."[124] The

---

120. Cf. Ibid., can. 536 § 1.

121. *Ecclesiae de Mysterio,* Practical Provisions, art. 5: loc. cit., pp. 867–868.

122. *Christifideles Laici,* 27; loc. cit., p. 441.

123. Ibid.

124. Sacred Congregation for the Clergy, Circular Letter *Omnes Christifideles* (January 25, 1973), 4; 9.

pastoral council is to be seen in relation to the context of the relationship of mutual service that exists between a parish priest and his faithful. It would therefore be senseless to consider the pastoral council as an organ replacing the parish priest in his government of the parish, or as one which, on the basis of a majority vote, materially constrains the parish priest in his direction of the parish.

In accordance with the norms of law on just and honest administration, organs which have been established to consider economic questions in a parish may not constrain the pastoral role of the parish priest, who is the legal representativc and administrator of the goods of the parish.[125]

Positive Contemporary Challenges for the Pastoral Ministry in Parishes

27. Since at the outset of the new millennium the entire Church has been invited to strive for "a renewed commitment to the Christian life," founded on an awareness of the risen Christ's presence among us,"[126] we must see the consequences of that invitation for pastoral care in parishes.

This does not require the invention of new pastoral programs, since the Christian program, revolving around Christ, is always one of knowing, loving and imitating him, of living the life of the Trinity in him, and of transforming history with him by bringing it to completion. "This is a program which does not change with shifts of times and cultures, even though it takes account of time and culture for the sake of true dialogue and effective communication."[127]

---

125. Cf. *CIC,* cann. 532, 1279, §1.

126. Cf. *Novo Millennio Ineunte,* 29: loc. cit., pp. 285–286.

127. Ibid.

In the immense and demanding pastoral horizons of today, "It is *in the local churches* that the specific features of a detailed pastoral plan can be identified—goals and methods, formation and enrichment of the people involved, the search for the necessary resources—which will enable the proclamation of Christ to reach people, mold communities, and have a deep and incisive influence in bringing Gospel values to bear in society and culture."[128] Such are the horizons of "an exciting work of pastoral revitalization—a work involving all of us."[129]

The most important and basic pastoral challenge facing the priest in the parish is to bring the faithful to a consistent spiritual life based on the principles of Christian doctrine as lived and taught by the saints. Pastoral planning must give priority to this essential aspect of all pastoral action. Today, more than ever, prayer, the sacramental life, meditation, silent adoration, talking heart to heart with the Lord, and daily exercise of the virtues which make us more like him must be rediscovered, since these are far more productive than any discussion, and ultimately the necessary condition for all effective discussion.

Novo Millennio Ineunte sets seven pastoral priorities: holiness, prayer, the Sunday celebration of the Most Holy Eucharist, the Sacrament of Penance, the primacy of grace, and listening to and proclaiming the Word.[130] These priorities became particularly clear from the experience of the Great Jubilee. Not only do they offer parish priests but all priests engaged in the *cura animarum* the content and substance of the pastoral questions on which they should carefully meditate. They also provide a

128. Ibid.
129. Ibid.
130. Ibid.

synthesis of the spirit with which the renewal of pastoral work should be approached.

Novo Millennio Ineunte also emphasizes another "important area in which there has to be commitment and planning on the part of the universal Church and the particular Churches: *the domain of communion (koinonia),* which embodies and reveals the very essence of the mystery of the Church" (n. 42) and implies the promotion of a spirituality of communion. "To make the Church *the home and the school of communion*: that is the great challenge facing us in the millennium which is now beginning, if we wish to be faithful to God's plan and respond to the world's deepest yearnings." Moreover, it also specifies that "before making practical plans, we need *to promote a spirituality of communion,* making it the guiding principle of education wherever individuals and Christians are formed, wherever ministers of the altar, consecrated persons, and pastoral workers are trained, wherever families and communities are being built up" (n. 43).

A truly pastoral promotion of the holiness of our parish communities implies an authentic pedagogy on prayer, a renewed, persuasive and effective catechesis on the importance of the Sunday and daily celebration of the Most Holy Eucharist, on community and personal adoration of the Blessed Sacrament, on the frequent and individual practice of the Sacrament of Penance, on spiritual direction, on Marian devotion, on the imitation of the saints, as well as on a renewed apostolic commitment to live the daily duties of the community and of individuals, proper pastoral care of the family, and on a consistent political and social engagement.

This pastoral renewal will not be possible unless inspired, sustained and activated by priests imbued by this same spirit. "The faithful draw great encouragement from the example and witness of the priest. They can rediscover the parish as a 'school' of prayer in which encounter with Jesus Christ is not merely expressed in implorings for assistance but also in acts of thanksgiving, praise, adoration, contemplation, prayerful listening, ardor of affection, to the point of truly loving him."[131] "It is fatal to forget that 'without Christ we can do nothing' (cf. Jn 15:5). It is prayer which roots us in this truth. It constantly reminds us of the primacy of Christ and, in union with him, the primacy of the interior life and of holiness. When this principle is not respected, is it any wonder that pastoral plans come to nothing and leave us with a disheartening sense of frustration? We then share the experience of the disciples in the Gospel story of the miraculous catch of fish: "We have toiled all night and caught nothing" (Lk 5:5). This is the moment of faith, of prayer, of conversation with God, in order to open our hearts to the tide of grace and allow the word of Christ to pass through us in all its power: *Duc in altum!*"[132]

A good laity is scarcely possible without truly holy priests. Without them everything is dead—just as it is almost impossible to have a blossoming of vocations without Christian families which are domestic churches. It is therefore erroneous to emphasize the laity if this entails overlooking the ordained ministry. Such error ends by penalizing the laity and frustrating the entire mission of the Church.

28. The rediscovery in our communities of the universal call to holiness should be the basis for all pastoral planning and

---

131. John Paul II, *Address to the Parish Priests and Clergy of Rome* (March 1, 2001), 3; cf. *Novo Millennio Ineunte,* 33: loc. cit., p. 289.

132. Ibid., 38: loc. cit., p. 293.

orient that same planning. The soul of every apostolate depends on divine intimacy, on placing nothing before the love of Christ, in seeking the greater glory of God in all things, in living the Christocentric dynamism of the Marian *"totus tuus." Training in holiness* "places pastoral planning under the sign of holiness"[133] and constitutes the primary pastoral challenge of contemporary times. In the holy Church, all of the faithful are called to holiness.

Teaching all, and recalling indefatigably, that holiness is the goal of Christian life is essential to the *pedagogy of holiness.* "All in the Church, whether they belong to the hierarchy or are cared for by it, are called to holiness, according to the Apostle's saying: 'For this is the will of God, your sanctification' (1 Thes 4:3; cf. Eph 1:3)."[134] This is the first element to be pedagogically developed in ecclesial catechesis, so that an awareness of the need for personal sanctification becomes a common conviction.

Proclamation of the universality of the call to holiness requires that the Christian life is understood as a *following of Christ,* or of being conformed to Christ. This conformation to Christ is the very substance of sanctification and is the specific goal of all Christian life. In order to accomplish this objective, all Christians need the Church's assistance, since she is both *mater et magistra*. The *pedagogy of holiness* is a goal which is as attractive as it is challenging for all those in the Church who hold responsibilities of government and formation.

29. A zealous missionary commitment to evangelization is a priority of singular importance for the Church and, conse-

---

133. Ibid., n. 31: loc. cit., p. 287.

134. *Lumen Gentium,* 39.

quently, for the pastoral care of the parish.[135] "Even in countries evangelized many centuries ago, the reality of a 'Christian society' which, amid all the frailties which have always marked human life, measured itself explicitly on Gospel values, is now gone. Today we must courageously face a situation which is becoming increasingly diversified and demanding, in the context of 'globalization' and of the consequent new and uncertain mingling of peoples and cultures."[136]

In contemporary society, which is marked by cultural, religious and ethnic pluralism, relativism, indifferentism, irenicism and syncretism, it appears that some Christians have become accustomed to a form of "Christianity" lacking any real reference to Christ and his Church. In these circumstances, the pastoral mission is reduced to social concerns which are envisaged in exclusively anthropological terms, often based on a vague appeal to pacifism, universalism or to a loose reference to "values."

The evangelization of the contemporary world can only happen with the rediscovery of the personal, social and cultural identity of Christians. That implies, above all else, the rediscovery of Jesus Christ, incarnate Word, and sole Savior of

---

135. Cf. Paul VI, Apostolic Exhortation *Evangelii Nuntiandi,* 14; John Paul II, *Address* to the Sacred Congregation for the Clergy (October 20, 1984): "Hence the need to rediscover the parish's specific function as a community of faith and charity, which is the reason for its existence and its most essential characteristic. That means making evangelization the axis of all pastoral activity since it is an urgent, preeminent and important demand. It is thus that a purely horizontal outlook of mere social presence is avoided, and it is thus that the Church's sacramental nature is reinforced" *(AAS* 77 [1984], pp. 307–308).

136. *Novo Millennio Ineunte,* 40: loc. cit., p. 294.

mankind.[137] This basic conviction sets free that missionary commitment which should especially characterize every priest, and through him, every parish or community entrusted to his pastoral care. "We hold that it is impossible even to imagine one pastoral method which is applicable to, or can be adapted to, all circumstances. Before us, this was axiomatic in the teaching of Gregory Nazianzus. A single pastoral method is excluded. In order to edify all in charity, it is necessary to vary the modes in which the hearts of faithful can be touched, but not doctrine. Pastoral care, therefore, requires an adaptation of modes but excludes any adaptation of doctrine."[138]

The parish priest will always ensure that the various associations, movements or groups present in the parish will make their specific contribution to the missionary endeavor of the parish. "Another important aspect of communion is *the promotion of forms of association,* whether of the more traditional kind or the newer ecclesial movements, which continue to give the Church a vitality that is God's gift and a true 'springtime of the Spirit.' Associations and movements in the Church, both at the universal and local level, must always operate in complete ecclesial harmony and obey the directives of their lawful pastors."[139] Every form of exclusivism or introspection among specific groups should be avoided in the parochial structure because its missionary character rests on the certainty, which should be shared by all, that "Jesus Christ has a significance and a value

137. Cf. Congregation for the Doctrine of the Faith, Declaration *Dominus Iesus* (August 6, 2000): *AAS* 92 (2000), pp. 742–765.

138. St. Gregory the Great, *Regula pastoralis,* Introduction to part three.

139. *Novo Millennio Ineunte,* 46: loc. cit., p. 299.

for the human race and its history, which are unique and singular, proper to him alone, exclusive, universal, and absolute. Jesus Christ is the Word of God made man for the salvation of mankind."[140]

The Church relies on the daily fidelity of her priests to the pastoral ministry as they attend to their indispensable mission in the parishes entrusted to their care.

For parish priests and other priests who serve various communities, certainly, there is no shortage of pastoral difficulties, or spiritual or physical exhaustion caused by overwork or a lack of that balance which recommends healthy periods of spiritual renewal and physical rest. What disappointments, it has to be stated, are experienced when the winds of secularism often choke the seeds sown with such noble daily effort.

A largely secularized culture which seeks to isolate the priest within its own conceptual categories and strip him of his fundamental mystical-sacramental dimension is largely responsible for this phenomenon. From this, several forms of discouragement can derive which lead to isolation, forms of depressive fatalism, and scattered activism. This, however, does not take from the fact that the vast majority of the Church's priests, supported by the solicitude of their bishops, face the difficulties of the present historical conjuncture positively, and succeed in joyfully living their generous pastoral commitment and their priestly identity to the full.

Internal dangers to the priestly ministry also exist: bureaucracy, functionalism, democratization, planning which is more managerial than pastoral. Unfortunately, in some circum-

---

140. *Dominus Iesus,* 15: loc. cit., p. 756.

stances, priests can be overwhelmed by structures which overpower them and are not always necessary, or which induce negative psycho-physical consequences detrimental for the spiritual life and for the very ministry itself.

The bishop is obliged carefully to be vigilant about such situations since he is, above all else, a father to his closest and most precious collaborators. It is both urgent and necessary to ensure unity among all ecclesial forces so as to respond effectively to the attacks currently being made on priests and their ministry.

30. In view of the current circumstances of the Church's life, the demands of new evangelization, and in consideration of the response which priests are called to make, the Congregation for the Clergy offers this present document as an aid for, an encouragement to, and a stimulus for the ministry of priests entrusted with the pastoral care of souls in parishes. Indeed, the Church's most immediate contact with people normally happens in the context of the parish. Our thoughts and considerations, therefore, are directed toward the priest *qua* parish priest. He represents the presence of Jesus Christ as head of his Mystical Body, the Good Shepherd who tends every single member of the flock. In this document, we have sought to highlight the mystery and sacramental nature of that ministry.

In the light of the teaching of the Second Vatican Council and the Apostolic Exhortation *Pastores Dabo Vobis,* this document should be seen as a continuity of the *Directory for the Ministry and Life of Priests,* the interdicasterial instruction *Ecclesiae de Mysterio,* and the circular letter *The Priest and the Third Christian Millennium, Teacher of the Word, Minister of the Sacraments and Leader of the Community.*

It is only possible to live the daily ministry by means of personal holiness, which should always be based on the supernatural power of the sacraments of the Holy Eucharist and Penance.

"The Eucharist is the point from which everything else comes forth and to which it all returns.... Through the centuries, countless priests have found in the Eucharist the consolation promised by Jesus on the evening of the Last Supper, the secret to overcoming their solitude, the strength to bear their sufferings, the nourishment to make a new beginning after every discouragement, and the inner energy to bolster their decision to remain faithful."[141]

Progress in the spiritual life and in permanent formation[142] can be greatly assisted by that fraternity among priests which is not merely one of simply being able to live together under the same roof, but one which involves communion of prayer, shared objectives, pastoral cooperation, and reciprocal friendship between priests and their bishop. This is also helpful in overcoming the trials and difficulties which are experienced in the exercise of the sacred ministry. Every priest not only needs the ministerial assistance of his own brethren, but also needs them precisely because they are his brethren.

Among other measures, a house could be set aside in the diocese for all priests who, from time to time, need to retire to a place suitable for recollection and prayer so as to renew contact with those means which are indispensable for their personal holiness.

In the spirit of the Cenacle, where the apostles gathered in prayer with Mary, the Mother of Jesus (Acts 1:14), to her we entrust these pages which have been written with affection and gratitude for all priests who exercise the *cura animarum* throughout the world. May all who are engaged in the pastoral

---

141. John Paul II, Letter to Priests on Holy Thursday 2000, 10, 14.
142. Cf. *Tota Ecclesia,* chapter III.

care of souls experience the maternal assistance of the Queen of Apostles and live in profound communion with her. The ministerial priesthood "has a stupendous and penetrating dimension in the closeness of the Mother of Christ [to priests]."[143] *It is a source of great consolation to know that "the Mother of the Redeemer who introduces us to the mystery of the redemptive offering of her divine Son, is always close to us. Ad Iesum per Mariam:* let this be the daily objective of our spiritual and pastoral life."[144]

The Supreme Pontiff John Paul II approved this present Instruction and ordered its publication.

Rome, at the offices of the Congregation for the Clergy, August 4, 2002, liturgical memorial of St. John Mary Vianney, Curé d'Ars, patron of parish priests.

+ Dario Cardinal Castrillon Hoyos
Prefect

+ Cesba Ternyak
Titular Archbishop of Eminenziana
Secretary

---

143. John Paul II, Letter to Priests on Holy Thursday 1979 *Novo Incipiente,* 11, loc. cit., p. 416.

144. John Paul II, *Address* to the Plenary Meeting: loc. cit., p. 217.

PARISH PRIEST'S PRAYER TO MARY MOST HOLY

O Mary, Mother of Jesus Christ, crucified and risen,
Mother of the Church, a priestly people (1 Pt 2:9),
Mother of priests, ministers of your Son:
accept the humble offering of myself,
so that in my pastoral mission
the infinite mercy of the Eternal High Priest
may be proclaimed:
O "Mother of Mercy."

You who shared the "priestly obedience" (Heb 10:5–7; Lk 1:38)
of your Son,
and who prepared for him a worthy receptacle
by the anointing of the Holy Spirit,
keep my priestly life in the ineffable mystery
of your divine maternity,
"Holy Mother of God."

Grant me strength in the dark hours of this life,
support me in the exertions of my ministry,
entrust me to Jesus,
so that, in communion with you,

I may fulfill the ministry with fidelity and love,
O Mother of the Eternal Priest,
"Queen of Apostles and Help of Priests."[145]

Make me faithful to the flock
entrusted to me by the Good Shepherd.
You silently accompanied Jesus
on his mission to proclaim
the Gospel to the poor.
May I always guide it
with patience, sweetness,
firmness and love,
caring for the sick,
the weak, the poor and sinners,
O "Mother, Help of the Christian People."

I consecrate and entrust myself to you, Mary,
who shared in the work of redemption
at the cross of your Son,
you who "are inseparably linked to the work of salvation."[146]
Grant that in the exercise of my ministry
I may always be aware of the "stupendous and penetrating dimension of your maternal presence"[147]
in every moment of my life,
in prayer and action,
in joy and sorrow, in weariness and in rest,
O "Mother of Trust."

---

145. *Presbyterorum Ordinis,* 18.

146. *Sacrosanctum Concilium,* 103.

147. John Paul II, Letter to Priests on Holy Thursday 1979 *Novo Incipiente,* 11, loc. cit., p. 416.

Grant, Holy Mother, that in the celebration of the Mass,
source and center of the priestly ministry,
I may live my closeness to Jesus
in your maternal closeness to him,
so that as "we celebrate the Holy Mass you will be present with us"
and introduce us to the redemptive mystery of your divine Son's offering,[148]
"O Mediatrix of all grace flowing from this sacrifice to the Church and to all the faithful,"[149]
O "Mother of Our Savior."

O Mary, I earnestly desire to place my person
and my desire for holiness
under your maternal protection and inspiration
so that you may bring me to that "conformation with Christ, Head and Shepherd"
which is necessary for the ministry of every parish priest.
Make me aware
that "you are always close to priests"
in your mission of servant
of the One Mediator, Jesus Christ:
O "Mother of Priests,"
"Benefactress and Mediatrix"[150]
of all graces.

Amen.

---

148. John Paul II, Address to the Plenary Meeting: loc. cit., p. 217.

149. John Paul II, On the Occasion of the Liturgical Memorial of Our Lady of Czestochowa, *L'Osservatore Romano,* August 26, 2001.

150. *Lumen Gentium,* 62.

ACT OF LOVE OF THE CURÉ D'ARS, ST. JOHN MARY VIANNEY

I love you, O my God, and my sole desire is to love you until the last breath of my life.

I love you, O infinitely lovable God, and I prefer to die loving you than live one instant without loving you.

I love you, O my God, and I do not desire anything but heaven so as to have the joy of loving you perfectly.

I love you, O my God, and I fear hell, because there will not be the sweet consolation of loving you.

O my God, if my tongue cannot say in every moment that I love you, I want my heart to say it in every beat. Allow me the grace to suffer loving you, to love you suffering and one day to die loving you and feeling that I love you. And as I approach my end, I beg you to increase and perfect my love of you.

The Daughters of St. Paul operate book and media centers at the following addresses. Visit, call or write the one nearest you today, or find us on the World Wide Web, www.pauline.org

California
3908 Sepulveda Blvd, Culver City, CA 90230 310-397-8676
5945 Balboa Avenue, San Diego, CA 92111 858-565-9181
46 Geary Street, San Francisco, CA 94108 415-781-5180

Florida
145 S.W. 107th Avenue, Miami, FL 33174 305-559-6715

Hawaii
1143 Bishop Street, Honolulu, HI 96813 808-521-2731
Neighbor Islands call: 800-259-8463

Illinois
172 North Michigan Avenue, Chicago, IL 60601 312-346-4228

Louisiana
4403 Veterans Memorial Blvd, Metairie, LA 70006 504-887-7631

Massachusetts
885 Providence Hwy, Dedham, MA 02026 781-326-5385

Missouri
9804 Watson Road, St. Louis, MO 63126 314-965-3512

New Jersey
561 U.S. Route 1, Wick Plaza, Edison, NJ 08817 732-572-1200

New York
150 East 52nd Street, New York, NY 10022 212-754-1110
78 Fort Place, Staten Island, NY 10301 718-447-5071

Pennsylvania
9171-A Roosevelt Blvd, Philadelphia, PA 19114 215-676-9494

South Carolina
243 King Street, Charleston, SC 29401 843-577-0175

Tennessee
4811 Poplar Avenue, Memphis, TN 38117 901-761-2987

Texas
114 Main Plaza, San Antonio, TX 78205 210-224-8101

Virginia
1025 King Street, Alexandria, VA 22314 703-549-3806

Canada
3022 Dufferin Street, Toronto, Ontario, Canada M6B 3T5 416-781-9131
1155 Yonge Street, Toronto, Ontario, Canada M4T 1W2 416-934-3440

¡También somos su fuente para libros, videos y música en español!